v v v

Shifting the Mind's Eye

v v v

Lorri Ventura

v v v

Photos accompanying the poems are by the author, except American Gothic by Grant Wood is from Wikimedia at the Google Cultural Institute.

About the Author

Lorri Ventura is a retired special education administrator based in Massachusetts, where she draws inspiration from the complexities of human experience. Her poetry has been widely published in esteemed journals such as AllPoetry, Mad Swirl, Massachusetts Bards, Parapraxis, Quabbin Quills, Red Eft Review, Wilderness House Literary Review, and Writing in a Woman's Voice. Ventura's work has received formal recognition, including three Moon Prize awards from Writing in a Woman's Voice.

Shifting the Mind's Eye, her debut poetry collection, marks a significant milestone in her literary journey. With unflinching candor and potent imagery, her poems grapple with the darker aspects of culture, family dynamics, trauma, and the search for solace. Her writing embodies a deep understanding of the human condition and the resilience that helps us process.

Contents

Woman In a Nursing Home

The skin on the backs of her hands
Looks like lady slipper petals
Translucent
Tiny-veined
So delicate
She scratches it incessantly
Buckled into a wheelchair
By the elevator door
In front of the nurses' station
Which is where the staff
Park the patients who don't get visitors
Threadbare pate pitched forward
Stained hospital gown doing its job half-heartedly
Covering body parts
That are faded memories
Of what they once were
Seemingly asleep
Until the elevator doors
Whisper their announcement
Of someone's arrival
Then, only then
Does she become animated
Her head lifts
Her smile is almost rictal
"Hi hi hi hi hi!"
She sing-songs

"See me!"
Her unspoken plea
I bend down
And carefully embrace her
Telling her she looks pretty today
Her fingers catch in my hair
Her skin smells like
Chicken grease
Rheumy eyes lock on mine
"Bless you bless you bless you!"
She warbles
It feels like a long time passes
Before we release each other
I think she just might be
The most inspiring human being
I've ever met

A Bostonian

His home is a rag-filled refrigerator box
Propped crookedly on broken sidewalk
Alongside the Boston Common

When I ask him his name
He says, "Just call me 'Least of Your Brothers,'
Then winks conspiratorially

He tugs off mismatched gloves
To jab his raw fingers
Into his tepid cup of Dunkin'
Before gulping its dregs

Coffee trickles through his beard
As he offers a sip from the empty cup
To a passerby
Who squawks in protest
Before bolting to the other side of Tremont Street

The gold-gilded State House dome
Shines down on him
As his gnarled fingers weave gently
Through the yarn hair of a grimy, one-eyed, Raggedy Ann
Propped in his lap

Every so often
He leans forward and kisses the top of the doll's head
With a sweetness that brings tears to my eyes

Seeing people turn their faces away
As they rush past
Pretending not to see him
He waves and grins lopsidedly
Showing three wobbly teeth and chortling,
"Smile! I won't hurt you! Have a nice day!"

I squint through the sunlight
As I watch him from the nearest corner
I think I see
A halo encircling his head.
#####

Two Tigers

Circling each other warily
Two tigers
In a cage built of
Deceit and grudges
Blowing on the embers
Of a union reduced to
An emotional junk drawer
Rifling through
Expired passion and broken communication
Clutching at sweetly scented memories
Apart together
Unhappily married couple

Heart of Haiti

His machete bobs lazily against his hip
As the old man shuffles up the mission house driveway
Hugging the armful of ungainly sticks he extends
An offering to the woman who squats on the ground by the fire
Stirring a pot brimming with rice and crushed peanuts drenched
in tabasco sauce

His dusty pants are held up by a belt made from yellowed banana leaves
On his feet he wears tire treads duct-taped to mismatched socks
He bows as he accepts a bowl of food
In exchange for the spindly firewood

We offer him a bedroll, a steaming mug of Re-Bo coffee, and a place to sit
But he just smiles and shakes his head
Tapping the raggedy pillowcase slung over his shoulder
As it holds all of his possessions
He waves an arm toward the sky
Telling us that he has everything he needs in the world
Before he bows and takes his leave

Predictable as ocean tide
The gentleman's silent appearance every day
As dinner is being served
Makes us smile
And wish that we could give him more

Deep down, though, we know
That already he has what makes him happy
Because he chooses to be happy with what he has.

Grandma Was a Medium

My grandmother talked to dead people
In the same tone of voice I used,
Years later,
When talking to my mother-in-law

Formality with a hint of burden

Quarantine Snapshots

Two shoppers
Engage in a tug-of-war
The prize
That last twelve-pack of Charmin

Miles from civilization, inverted rubber gloves
And muddied surgical masks
Become ominous blue flecks
Littering the hiking trails

A bedridden senior
Stares out a window
Willing the arrival of family
Who cannot visit

A world in which heroes
Wear surgical scrubs
Drive delivery trucks
Teach their children at home
Stack canned goods

A planet in corrective action

Domestic Violence

Daddy shot the family dog
Because it looked at him the wrong way
Mommy's ribs
Like two rows of broken wishbones
In the x-ray

Shut up, little girl
And swallow the Benadryl
So you can sleep through the yelling
Fifty-five years later
Oral meds still taste like terror and rage

Those are just baby teeth
It's okay that Daddy knocked them out
You'll grow new ones
And he had a rough day at work
Poor Daddy

Daddy's handgun lived on the hutch
Always oiled
Always loaded
Often brandished in our faces
To keep us in our places

Pray, sweet child of mine, Mommy said, You are my angel
Daddies can't kill angels
They just like to try
The little girl refused to pray to a God
Who sees without helping

Mom

Born on St. Joseph's feast day
She hoped to merit his protection
And she lived,
Until she didn't.
Her spirit drifted away
Writhing
In the smoke
Of the cigarettes
She puffed obsessively

Paupers Cemetery

Turkey vultures
Venture beyond a nearby landfill
Circling evocatively above the paupers' graves
On Mayflower Hill.

Grave markers resemble key heads
Bearing not names, but numerals
A potter's field
Stretching from a trash-strewn roadside to a forest

Unnamed graves embrace the insane
Forced to sew their own burial shrouds

While hunched on cots
In the nearby state hospital

Alongside them are infants and children
Resting eternally with strangers
In group plots
To conserve space

The earth comforts the nameless poor
Their dreams curtailed by monsters
Bearing melodic names—
Diphtheria, Dropsy, Dysentery, Dementia, Despair

Beneath numbered iron markers
Lie the forgotten, abandoned, and lost
Lives perhaps un-noted
But not without value

Sixth Station of the Cross

First Fridays were for praying
At the stations of the cross
The petite young mother
Chapel cap pinned to her hair
Rosary beads clicking against her fingernails

She pulls along her little girl
Whose rubber-soled Buster Browns
Squeak the entire length of the tiled church aisle
While she twirls her ponytails
And practices crossing her eyes
To make the time pass more quickly

But when they arrive at the sixth station
The little girl always forgets her boredom
And stares at the image of Veronica
Wiping Jesus' face with a cloth
His visage appears on the fabric
The way the funnies in the newspaper
Slide onto her Silly Putty
When she presses it against the newsprint

The child is drawn to this station
Because it shows a female
Doing something important
This legend somehow gives her hope
For her own future

At home, she gingerly presses a washcloth
Against her Chatty Cathy's face
Pretending the doll's upturned nose and freckles
Materialize on the terrycloth

The child becomes a woman
Who passes judgment on the Church
That itself has judged and excluded so many
Yet she clings to her belief that the Divine
Lives within all
And that the image shown on Veronica's cloth
Shines within us whenever we show love
*

Humpty Dumpty: A Story of Recovery

(Humpty Dumpty sat on a wall
Humpty Dumpty had a great fall
All the king's horses and all the king's men
Couldn't put Humpty together again)

So up Humpty got
A quitter he was not!
He mended his shell
And, in time, he felt well

Recovery was slow
Each setback, a blow
But when he stood tall
A role model to all

"Hard work is worthwhile,"
He said with a smile
Don't embrace defeat
Unless it's to repeat

Each crack told a story
Of Humpty's return to glory
His tale can come true
For me, and for you

Ode to My Husband

Countless kisses later
My lips still delight
In the thrill yours brings to them

Estate Sale

A cluster of dust-covered Hummels
Surround a Japanese puzzle box
Hand-knitted sweaters in toppling piles
Reek of cigarette smoke

Stacks of carnival glass dishware
Playfully cast rainbow prisms on faded walls
Dozens of boxes bulge with books
And sheet music

Sepia photos
With curled edges
Share unsmiling faces
Long gone

Crowds of barterers
Seek the adrenalin rush
They get from
Successful low-balling
For items they can resell
At a profit

Memory-triggering tchotchkes
More trash than treasure
Vestigial remains
Of a priceless life

A Child's Dreams

In her dreams she drives an ice cream truck
And hands free fudgsicles to all the children
She cures cancer
Ends wars
Reverses climate change
And speaks all languages fluently.
She spreads kernels of beauty and hope
Wherever she goes
The way Miss Rumphius blanketed the earth
With lupine seeds
Best of all
She lives in a house full of cats
That purr her to sleep at night
So that she can save the world

-

Barn Spider

Pre-dawn moonbeams kiss her web
As she waits, poised to pounce
When a moth flutters haplessly
Toward her gossamer labyrinth.

Her black and amber body
Clings, motionless, to her cat's cradle,
Which shimmers in one corner of a hayloft window.

Her barnyard companions
Nicker, stomp, snort, and crow,
Restlessly signaling their hunger,
Eagerness for the sun to rise,
And need for acknowledgment.

The barn spider, though, knows
That no one will come to feed, groom,
Or greet her.
Serenely she waits for her intricate handiwork
To ensnare her meal.

A model of humility and self-sufficiency,
The arachnid shows us
That hard work and perseverance,
Often unnoticed,
Bring fulfillment

The Tin Dollhouse

Life never changes
Inside the tin dollhouse.
Mommy stands in the kitchen,
Eternally offering lunchboxes
To her two smiling children,
Permanently clad in their best school clothes.
She does not have to fear
That her beloved babies
Will be shot in their classrooms.

Daddy poses forever
On the kelly green metal lawn,
Attached to the hose he aims
At the ever-blooming zinnias
Painted along the house's side.
He does not worry that unrestrained
Expulsion of pollutants
Will contaminate his garden,
The unending stream of water,
Gushing from his hose,
Or the air he breathes.

A plastic woman walks her silicone dog
Past the tin dollhouse
With no concerns that a government
Will steal her reproductive rights,
Persecute her for the color of her skin,

For whom she loves,
Or how she worships.

Leaning in a doorway
Beyond the tin dollhouse
A mother gazes at her little girl,
Crouched on the floor,
Peering into each miniature room.
She sighs softly
And wishes her daughter's world were as safe and just
As the one embodied by her toy.

Soul of the Mekong

The Mekong River hums
Happy to host the morning's floating market
A woman stands tall
In her dilapidated sampan

Sun's rays dance
Atop her non la hat
Wisps of gray hair wave beneath its cone
She poles deftly
Through a cluster of similar vessels
None look water-worthy
Yet all bob jauntily
Their bows decorated with brightly colored eyeballs
Painted there to ensure a safe homecoming
The woman's sampan groans
With the weight of baskets made from water hyacinths
Overflowing with freshly-harvested rambutans
Red, eyelashed fruits
Vietnamese treasures
Nearby, a boy squats in a sampan laden with chilies and bananas
And a family offers pimply-skinned guavas from a vessel
That wobbles, low and heavy in the river
All nod respectfully as the old woman glides past
She greets no one
Yet blesses everyone she passes
Her skin as silt-colored as the river she commands
The spirit of the Mekong shines through her eyes

Hermit in the Woods

Despite the rumor that she ate children
I looked for her
As I rode my horse along the overgrown, old, lumberjack trail.
Once I saw her drifting toward me among the towering oaks
At first I thought she was a rag-clad ghost
Her skin translucent
Waist-length hair colorless
And adorned with brown leaves.
Nostrils flared,
My palomino shied away from her fusty odor.
As if possessed,
I slowly reached into my saddle bag.
Hands trembling,
I held out the carrot packed
As a treat for my mount.
The woman crept toward me
Then, fast as a beam of light,
She grabbed with a vine-like hand,
And devoured the root tuber.
Subtly tugging on the bridle's reins,
I backed up,
Worried that the specter was eyeing me
As her lunch entree.
But then she dropped to her knees,
Head bowed and hands clasped as if in prayer
Giving me both leave and benediction.

I never told my parents,
Knowing that they'd forbid me ever again to ride in the forest
But whenever I rode down that path
I packed an extra sandwich or snack
In case the woman re-appeared.
Never again did she grace me with her presence
No matter how hard I searched.

Filipino Symphony

Pink plastic bowls overflow with chicken feet
Ready for marination in brown sugar and spices,
Destined for transformation into a popular street food dubbed
"Adidas"
After the athletic footwear.

Children waving paper fans
Swat at orange-eyed flesh flies
Using the fowl feet as landing strips

Three hundred varieties of rice,
More colorful than rainbows.

Purses made from massive, olive-drab frogs
Copper zippers holding their mouths closed.

Long lines of customers
Queue to purchase civet coffee,
A Filipino specialty brewed from
Java beans swallowed whole by an exotic feline and then excreted,
Enhanced by the fermentation of their digestive experience.

Acacia carvings—
Everything from furniture to phalluses
In heartwarming browns and reds.
Wafer cones dripping with purple ice cream
Made from yams.

In the center of an aisle lined with
Bird whistle toys and cloth dolls
A handprinted sign points toward a ladder
That reaches upward to a dental office
Where patients can enjoy discounted tooth extractions
And also adopt rheumy-eyed puppies
That wiggle and yip in a chewed, rattan basket
At the office entrance

Clusters of tailors
Race their antediluvian sewing machines
As they make tribal-patterned clothes "while-you-wait".
Vendors sing of their wares and
Tug at the arms of passersby
In their quest to be noticed.

In a dark alcove
Huddled between two looming trash dumpsters
A soot-covered old woman sits with a lapful of emaciated kittens.

She smiles and blows kisses to the crowds
Who throng past.
The woman's arms wave,
One reflecting emotion
The other seeming to keep the market's beat,
Conducting the symphony
That is the marketplace.

#

City Snapshot

A minefield of homeless people
Strewn like pickup sticks
Across the pavement
On the brick and concrete sidewalks
Of Central Square
Shoppers zigzag around them
With their eyes locked on their cell phones
To avoid truly seeing
Those less fortunate than they
Cocooned in layers of raggedy cardigans
A spavined woman sprawls along a bench
Clutching the matted fur
Of a pumpkin-colored cat
Curled, Cheeto-like,
Against her torso
A bearded man
Lost in billowing, cookie dough camouflage pants
Lurches forward in a wheelchair
That seems to be held together
By bumper stickers
He extends a coffee-stained paper cup
Toward passersby
Hoping for charity
Chuckling, he points to the largest decal
Its message:
"So many pedestrians, so little time."

A trio of laughing college students
Engrossed in conversation
Trample on a potholder-crocheted afghan
That a young girl has spread out on the sidewalk
To define the boundaries of her "home"
She glares up
Spitting profanities at the oblivious trespassers
Her peers in age if not in fortune
And brusquely swats at the footprints
Left on her most precious possession

Dickensian scenes in the 21st century
Mock our claims of social enlightenment
Expose our lack of humaneness
And beg us all to wake up

America in 1952

Mr. Potato Head is a real potato
Festooned with purchased plastic facial features.
Ralph Kramden drives a Brooklyn bus
In search of happiness.

The birth rate is double what it was ten years earlier.
Relishing post-war prosperity,
Americans are mass consumers of all things material.
Owning a suburban home
Has become more affordable
Than renting a city tenement.
A nation economically unrivaled!

Life is simpler
Happier
Sweeter now
Than ever before
Our descendants will reflect longingly
On "the good old days"
And call us blessed

But women in 1952
Cannot sell or buy property,
Control their own earnings,
Or draft their own wills

Children of color
Cannot attend a well-resourced
Integrated public school
And fewer than two of every ten black children
Have the opportunity to graduate from high school

Youngsters with disabilities
Languish at home
Public school doors closed to them
Or live, warehoused, in institutions
Isolated from their families

Paupers
Petty criminals
Persons with mental illness
Subsist, quartered in dungeon-like facilities
Sterilized, lobotomized
To make life easier for the rest of us

People suspected of engaging in homosexual behavior
Are denied jobs and housing
And the United States Post Office
Reads our mail, destroying
Any missives that hint of gay content

Rosy retrospection
Focusing on a decade
Of unprecedented growth
At the expense of our most vulnerable citizens

Paints a false picture
Of "good old days" that never were.

#

Old House

Awaiting demolition
The vacant house sags tiredly on its lot
Cracked window panes stare defeatedly at a bulldozer
Creeping steadily forward on lawn-lacerating tracks
In its final moments, the aged structure conjures ghosts
As faded as the stained, peeling wallpaper
Visions of children splash raucously, sloppily,
In its pink tiled bathroom.
Doors slam in anger
And burst open in welcome.
Sunbeams tickle the faces of late sleepers.
At holiday gatherings
Families crowd first at the kitchen table
And then around the piano.
The abode feels sapped but satisfied
With the knowledge that it served well.
Today the house takes its final measure.
It creaks its hardwood floors, gouged by cleated footwear
Jostles moth-eaten Persian carpets rolled up against the walls
Shakes its mouse dropping-covered countertops.
Wriggles the wires that dangle above each room as testament
To the former locations of ceiling lights.
Sections of its framework are torn off,
Mourned by now useless nails that protrude, dagger-like,
Menacing the passage between living and dining rooms.
The house quakes with the weight of memories.

The bulldozer's inexorable approach
Warns the old house that it is time
For surrender to the future —
A trophy home intended to impress.
The once venerable homestead heaves one last shudder
(An onlooker swears she hears it sigh.)
As the mighty machine relentlessly pushes
Up against its outer walls
Then, with a mighty roar that sounds somehow celebratory,
The old house collapses.

Sanctuary

The moon drops into the child's black-and-blue arms
Nestling there contentedly
As the little girl bobs across her backyard
Limps up the steps leading to her house
And ducks into her under-the-stairs bedroom
(A converted broom closet)
She gently tosses the orb into the air
Where it joins the stars she has collected
On previous nights
The closet suddenly transforms into a peaceful paradise
Deer graze in the gloaming
Fireflies kiss the child's nose before dancing away
A snowy owl perches on a tree branch
Serving as sentinel
The little girl scrambles into her bed
Satisfied that the world she has imagined
Will keep her safe from the dangers
That lurk in the chaotic reality
On the other side of the closet door
She falls asleep smiling

Ode to Those in a Trauma Center Waiting

Room

Together alone
While their loved ones undergo medical procedures
They stare blindly at a crookedly mounted TV
Offering soap operas at full-volume

They fan through dog-eared pages
Of months old People magazines
And gnaw on ragged fingertips
As their lips dance with anxious prayers

Around them, an intercom crackles
Calling color codes
That trigger storms of scrubs, lab coats
And rattling service carts
Flashing past

They pace back and forth
Across threadbare carpeting
In front of an aquarium
Filled with colorful tropical fish
Placed there to provide cheer and diversion
But ominously message-laden
With two rotund goldfish
Floating upside down at the water's surface

They pretend not to see the people
Who share the crowded room with them
Each one emotionally alone and unprepared

Like those in the throes of surgery
Those who wait
Hover between life and death

Matriarch

Subsisting on sufferance
She's a jumble of ideas
With hopes and fears
And challenges
Consuming many years.
She sits alone and silent
Made invisible by age
Once a vibrant woman
In her dotage she feels beige
She has no personality
Or so she thinks, alas,
Her children grown and far away
How swiftly time did pass!
No stranger to adversity
As strong as tempered steel
A single mom, she raised her young
Their success made her feel real.
Nurturing others' achievements
She rarely saw her own
Which tower like a mountain
Adding gravitas to her tone.
Her family exists as photos
Tacked up on a bedroom wall
Grandchildren! Great-grands!
Held up by tape
She hasn't met them all.

Like an ember growing cold
Her light begins to flicker
As with advancing age
Her body becomes sicker.
But an ember, humble though it seems
Can sail upon a breeze
And share its heat while dark it grows
To inspire, guide, appease

Old Dog

Dozing on a fur-festooned sofa
One floppy ear turned inside out
Paws periodically twitching
Flews flapping with each snore
A snuggly, smelly antidote
To whatever ails me

Glimmer of Hope

As we careen toward the edge of an abyss
The revelation that our countrymen have chosen
To support hatred, lies, and discrimination
In the hopes of obtaining lower prices
For butter and eggs
Cannot break our spirits
Unless we permit it to do so

The far-reaching ripples of a single pebble
In a pond remind us
That even the smallest among us
Can make a positive impact
And together, we can drive change
With unwavering kindness and love

Not in My Backyard

The woven chaise lounge creaks its protest
As I shift my weight
While turning the page of the book I'm reading

The backyard offers a symphony
A Carolina wren serenades from its perch on a nearby deck rail
Chickadees excitedly announce their discovery of a full bird
feeder
And mourning doves coo a conversation

Overhead, the sky is a graph of condensation trails
Transforming me into a vertex
For jets flying to and from
Both Boston and Providence

As I gaze up at the cerulean sky
Its puffy clouds part
And spotlight my sister in a migrant camp
Two days without food or water
Blistered lips and feet
Desiccating in scorching sun
Waiting, waiting, waiting
For a court date to hear her asylum petition

Peering past the dust at our nation's border
I see a barefoot sister in Gaza
Stumbling through bombed-out ruins

Of the hospital where she delivered her firstborn
Just seven days earlier.
She cannot find her baby.

Further ahead the clouds reveal
A sister in Ukraine
Formerly a school teacher
She now works 14-hour shifts
As a boiler operator
Dreaming of the day
When her school is rebuilt and reopened
And her husband is home from war.

From the comfort of my solitary paradise
Tears wobble down my cheeks
As I squint up at my sisters
Knowing they all deserve everything I have.

Life in a Family Shelter

Signs posted on every window sill
Reminders to please, please not toss
Dirty diapers out onto the lawn
Toilet paper kept in locked cabinets
Permission required to access a roll
Eight families sharing one kitchen
A screaming match triggered by
A soup ladle's disappearance
Eleven children sniffle and sneeze
With a shared head cold
A little girl turns somersaults
On a graffiti-bedecked This End Up couch
As two toddlers, arms linked, share a lollipop
On a frayed carpet in front of a TV
Watching "Paw Patrol" at full volume
And a boy caped in a bath towel
Tears up and down the hallway
The world's cutest Super Man
A young mom plants a bouquet of sleepy kisses on her baby's
head
Grease stains on her red Arby's apron
Nighttime descends
A mother forms a comma around her child
On the cot they share
And falls asleep
Dreaming of a world in which a full-time job

Stocking Wal-Mart shelves
Pays enough for an apartment
And for peace of mind

Lives on Pause

Unfinished

First lines of unwritten poems
Scamper through my head
Ledes with hooks that pull a reader into their embrace
But then
Fizzle in the absence of a second line
Partial poems are metaphors for my life
Unrealized hopes and unfinished projects
The faded segment of a baby blanket I began knitting
To welcome the birth of my first daughter
Who now is 37 years old
The piano lessons I've wanted to take
Since childhood
Although I still haven't gotten around
To buying a piano
The vacations I fantasized
About taking my kids on
If I weren't a cash-strapped
Single parent
Symbols of dreams derailed and deferred
And yet my life's loose ends
Have melded into a potpourri
In which the bitter scents
And those that were not part of the original recipe
Add as much to the medley's richness
As the vibrant, carefully orchestrated aromas
This gives me hope that my many

Poetic false starts
Might do the same :-)

On Grant Wood's "American Gothic"

An ekphrastic poem inspired by Grant Wood's famous artwork

Gripping a pitchfork as if it were Poseidon's trident
A farmer glares eternally from a world in turmoil
While his daughter's sidelong glance
Hints at her longing to escape
A hardscrabble existence
In Iowa during the Great Depression
An imposing window beckons ironically
From a flimsy Sears Roebuck house
While a potted mother-in-law's tongue on the porch
Personifies the indomitable hardiness of the pioneers
Who placed it there

Haiku

The last man standing
After the apocalypse
Regrets surviving

Haiku

Tears coursed down His cheeks
As he gazed at the remains
Of what once was Earth

Haiku

If Heaven is real
It is filled with books and cats
And my mom lives there

Haiku

The Christmas tree tilts
Ornaments fly through the air
Where could our cat be???

Haiku

In order to read
I need a cat on my lap
Rhythmically purring

www.ingramcontent.com/pod-product-compliance
Lightning Source LLC
Chambersburg PA
CBHW072246010125
19775CB00026B/238

9 798300 696337